Contents

SHELLEY'S SHACKLES

A Journey through the Juvenile Justice System

This book is intended to be used as a reference or guide to help family and friends understand the various stages of the juvenile justice system as it pertains to a new detainee. The information contained in this booklet has been condensed and generalized to be useful within all states.

The Department of Juvenile Justice (DJJ) is a government agency with offices located throughout the United States. This agency reports directly to the State Governor.

DJJ's mission is to increase public safety by reducing juvenile delinquency through effective prevention, intervention and treatment services that strengthens families and turn around the lives of troubled youth.

The Agency is committed to working with children, families, schools, law enforcement and communities to prevent youth from getting into trouble with the law; providing care and treatment according to youth's needs; supervising youth according to court orders; working with courts to hold youth responsible for their actions; determining what help each youth and family might need; helping youth make better choices; and providing the **4 R's – right services, in the right place, at the right time and in the right way.**

Shelley looks around the courtroom as she and her fellow inmates were marched to their assigned seating. The courtroom is filled with spectators, as well as, the attorneys, bailiffs and other regular court personnel. The low rumble of voices is like thunder to Shelley's ears. She didn't sleep well last night and her head is throbbing. Shelley's shackles are hurting her ankles. Her handcuffs are a bit tight, too, but she has learned that comfort is not a priority here.

Shelley looks for her Mother in the crowd – she's always here. Maybe this time she has really had enough. She told Shelley at her last visit to the detention center that she was tired of trying to tell Shelley that her behavior absolutely needed changing and that she was surely headed for prison, if she didn't "straighten up and fly right!"

Shelley began to feel anxious and alone. She needs her Mother. At that moment, Shelley caught her Mother's eye and she gave Shelley a crooked smile. She was there, as always. She supports her daughter – no matter what. Shelley breathed a sigh of relief and felt a bit comforted by her mom's presence.

There is a hush over the courtroom as the judge enters.

 "All rise!"

Judge Stiffneck is known as a stern but fair judge. Shelley sure hopes he's having a good day! Shelley can't believe how far she has fallen down this rabbit hole. It seems like only yesterday she was a young, carefree and energetic little girl with a bright future ahead of her. Shelley's thoughts become scattered as she tries to listen to the courtroom drama and reminisce about her younger days and what has brought her here.

THE BEGINNING
A BULLYING CULTURE

Shelley remembers being a pretty good student in elementary school – not all A's, but B's and C's and the occasional A. She was well liked by all her teachers. But junior high was the beginning of the bullying behavior that Shelley was soon to become a part of. She was the target of the boys bullying her because of her physical stature – she was not only taller than most of her classmates, but she had "filled out" earlier than most of the girls. The teasing was re-lentless. But she discovered that if she be-came the bully towards someone else, it took the attention away from her. So, bully-ing became her main goal in junior high. She remembered a young girl being bullied to the point of her taking her own life. Shel-ley remembers her because she was one of the main ones taunting and teasing her mercilessly.

The culture of bullying was rampant in her school, as she recalls. There were teachers who were as bad as the kids, as far as, name calling. Ms. Crumble would call you a "dummy" in a hot minute! Shelley remembers one kid, Peter? Pe-ter something – she can't recall the name now – but she remembers his tormented little face. He had a break out of eczema on his face and he was teased beyond tears – he started to fight and misbehave and eventually was expelled from school.

The victim became the offender.

The crowd that Shelley began to run with went on to not just bullying but fighting, stealing and all manner of destructive behavior. Then came the arrests for petty crimes (misdemeanors)– shoplifting, battery and others.

 In the beginning, Shelley was released to her Mother but as the destructive behavior escalated, so did the punishment. She was put on home detention which means being

in the custody of her Mother but with restrictions and DJJ supervision. Shelley was
given many chances to correct her behavior
but the bullying culture was now part of her
DNA.

FIRST FELONY

Felony – a crime, typically one involving violence,
regarded as more serious than a misdemeanor,
and usually punishable by imprisonment for more
than one year or by death.

 Shelley and her friends thought it would be
cool to steal a car. The easiest thing to do.
People leave keys in their cars all the time,
especially if parked in the driveway or garage. They would only keep it for a few hours

and then dump it somewhere. Possibly drive it until it runs out of gas – then ditch it.

So, Shelley and her gang cruise a neighborhood one afternoon until they spotted a car in an open garage and decided this was the perfect setup. They had seen a mother get out with her baby and scramble inside. They also saw her put the keys on a peg near the entrance. The gang stopped and watched to see if she would return or at least close the garage doors. She didn't. "Boy! This was just too easy. People sure are dumb," thought Shelley.

The gang was joy-riding 20 miles away when they were stopped by the sheriffs. Shelley wasn't driving but she was in the stolen car. Her first felony - grand theft auto.

THE ARREST

The officer that pulled them over was very stern and when they were told to get out of the car, they knew he meant business. There Shelley was – face down on the side of the road for all passers-by to gawk at her. What would her mother think? Lately Shelley's mother has had a hard time disciplining her. She looks and acts like an adult – but she still has a child's mentality. But Shelley surely knows right from wrong.

Her mother also knows Shelley is headed down a path that she is sure to regret.

The officer calls for backup and the two cars transport the gang directly to the Juvenile Assessment Center.

JUVENILE ASSESSMENT CENTER

 At the JAC, Shelley and her companions are assessed and processed. There they are fingerprinted, pictures taken, assigned identifying numbers and relieved of their possessions, including their clothing.

They are interviewed and information about them and their *alleged* crimes are entered into the Department of Juvenile Justice's state computer system.

 Shelley has been here before, so her file will be updated using her unique identifying number. Her companions are first offenders and will be assigned identifying number and inducted into the Juvenile Justice System. They all now have juvenile records.

The juveniles' next of kin are notified of their whereabouts.

JUVENILE DETENTION CENTER

INITIAL SCREENING

During the first 24 hours, there are Mental Health Assessments, as well as, Medical Health Assessments. These highly trained personnel will make a complete report of the youth and his case to make the best rec-ommendation to the court. They will decide whether youth is likely to show up for court and stay out of further trouble or if he is a menace to himself and others.

MEDICAL HEALTH ASSESSMENT

Medical evaluations are taken of youth – personal and family medical histories, vitals, weight, height, vision, etc. Pregnancy tests are given to females. Medical personnel are on-site 7 days a week to assist youth with medications, if needed.

MENTAL HEALTH ASSESSMENT

Mental assessments will include suicide precautions, sexual victimization and other pertinent mental assessments such as substance abuse and psychiatric disorders. Mental health personnel are available 7 days a week.

ASSIGNMENT OF QUARTERS

Male and female detainees live in separate living quarters with a common area for socialization. There are separate holding cells for those in need of total separation from the rest of the population. Cells are basic and sparse – usually only a place for sleeping and a toilet.

CAFETERIA

Nutritious and balanced meals are prepared on-site and served in the dining area daily.

SCHOOLING

While in the care of DJJ, youth are encouraged to continue their schooling. There are scheduled classroom times with state approved curriculums.

LIBRARY

There are several activities and services available, including an array of library books tailored for all ages and comprehension levels.

VOLUNTEERS

 Volunteer activities such as gardening, art, motivational speaking and music are provided, as well. The facilities are always looking for ways to help engage the youth with positive outside influences.

GUARDIAN AD LITEM

Guardian ad Litem volunteers stand up for the best interests of children who have been abused or neglected. Appointed by judges, they speak up for the child's needs in the courtroom and the community.

RECREATION

 The youth are given regular opportunities for recreation inside and outside on the facility grounds. Basketball and board games are very popular.

DETENTION HEARING

 A Detention Hearing must be held within 24 hours following a juvenile's arrest. Those released to parents and those in a juvenile detention center must be present. A judge will make sure every youth has an attorney, knows his or her rights and what he or she is charged with. The judge finalizes the temporary placement of youth at a detention center; or on home detention; or possibly releasing youth with charges being dropped. There aren't any pleas at this hearing.

Arresting Officer – the arresting officer has the discretion that allows him to decide if he wants to pursue police procedure and arrest (seize someone by legal authority and take them into custody) or simply let someone off with a warning. These officers are sometimes present at detention hearings after filing a complaint with the court and will now be a witness, if necessary. The arresting officer's absence **is not** an automatic reason to drop an arrest charge.

State Attorney's Office (also Commonwealth's Attorney; District Attorney) – the state attorney is a lawyer representing the interest of the state in a legal proceeding, typically as a prosecutor. The prosecution is the legal party responsible for presenting the case against an individual suspected of breaking the law.

Their duties generally include charging crimes through an *Information*. The State Attorney reviews DJJ reports and decides whether to file and then recommends to the judge what the charges and consequences should be.

Often charges are filed but the youth must only participate in a program and not have to appear in court again; or charges are filed and youth must appear later before a judge; and sometimes there are no charges filed and youth's case is dismissed.

Juvenile Probation Officers (JPO's) - The juvenile probation officer supervises youth who have been accused or convicted of crimes and are subsequently placed on probation or under protective supervision.

JPO's work closely with DJJ, law enforcement, social services, schools, and parents to help juveniles become successful. A primary duty for a probation officer is to meet with his assigned offenders on a weekly or monthly basis. The court designates how often each offender must meet with his officer. At these meetings, the officer reviews the requirements established for the probation. In addition, the probation officer spends a great deal of time performing work for the courts.

They are tasked with performing thorough background research on the offender; after compiling their findings, they write a pre-sentence document, and recommend a feasible sentence. The probation officer is also responsible for keeping the court current on the compliance of the offender with the court issued mandates.

Equipping probation and parole officers with firearms is becoming an increasingly common practice and many states arm these officers as a matter of officer safety. After all, probation and parole officers are out in the community, visiting parolees on their "home turf", which puts officers in vulnerable and often dangerous situations.

In many cases, these officers are in the community alone, and do not have direct support from fellow officers. Therefore, it's critical for officers to be able to protect themselves from the often-violent offenders they're tasked with supervising.

Lawyers (Counsel) - Everyone going to court must be represented by legal counsel. A criminal defense lawyer, also known as a defense attorney, is a lawyer specializing in the defense of individuals and companies charged with criminal conduct.

Some criminal lawyers are privately retained, while others are employed by the various jurisdictions with criminal courts for appointment to represent indigent persons; the latter are generally called public defenders.

If a youth and/or their family cannot afford a private attorney, a public defender will be appointed.

ARRAIGNMENT HEARING

With his lawyer, the youth now tells the judge whether he is "guilty" or is "not guilty" of the alleged charges against him.

If youth pleads "not guilty" during his arraignment hearing, the judge will schedule a trial for a later date to allow time for gathering information about youth's background from DJJ. If at trial the youth is found guilty, he will have a disposition hearing to decide what youth's punishment should be.

If a youth pleads "guilty" during his arraignment hearing, the judge can sentence him right away or wait and decide on his consequences during another disposition hearing.

A "plea bargain" may be presented to the judge in "not guilty and "no contest" pleas.

This means the state attorney's office, public defender or private attorney, and the youth have already met and agreed to what should happen in his case.

The Juvenile Court Judge - Juvenile court judges are responsible for hearing court cases and serving the best interests of the offenders, victims and communities. Juvenile courts handle matters involving minors under age 18.

Juvenile court judges may hear witness testimony and review reports submitted by the juvenile probation department and DJJ.

These judges must consider the seriousness of the crime and past criminal history. Juvenile judges must also consider factors such as age, home life and school behavior when making decisions about juvenile cases.

The judge will decide if he agrees with the temporary placement of a youth in a detention facility or at home with or without restrictions – which could sometimes mean wearing an electronic monitor.

 Shelley has been through the System on four separate occasions. Each time she falls deeper and deeper into that dark hole. Her mother has practically given up on her. Her Juvenile Probation Officer (JPO) has coun-seled her on many occasions to no avail. Shelley does what Shelley wants.

Each time she was in detention, she became more and more disruptive than the first. She has become accustomed to the revolv-ing door of the system. She knows she only must stay in a few days or weeks at a time. No big deal. Except, Shelley will soon be eighteen and her times spent in juvenile detention will be coming to an end. Shelley has promised her Mom and JPO that she will make a true effort to turn her life around before she ends up in prison for the rest of her life. Her Guardian ad Litem has bent over backwards trying to help steer Shelley in the right direction. But Shelley's promises are hollow – Shelley thinks she knows the system well enough to stay clear of any charges that would net her any serious time. Shelley is too smart for that.

Shelley and her friend have now become in possession of a gun. They bought it off another kid who swiped it from his old man's closet. Shelley's not sure she wants to be in possession of a gun - she refuses to carry it.

THE RABBIT HOLE (2ND FELONY)

 It was only supposed to be for show but something went awfully wrong one fateful night. It was Christmastime and there are always lots of ways to get some quick cash. Stealing packages from doorsteps is as easy as it gets. But the real money is in the mall parking lots – loads of packages and fat wallets.

Shelley and her friend decided to take their new gun on one of their shoplifting sprees. Shelley didn't want to have possession of the gun – seeing as she was only a few months from becoming eighteen years of age. When emancipated by the courts, she will be tried as an adult and would be treated as such if she was ever seen in

Judge Stiffneck's court again – EVER. So, her friend carried the gun.

In the parking garage there was an older gentleman and woman carrying packages – the perfect prey. Shelley snatched and grabbed the large bag from the woman's hand and ran – waiting for her friend to do the same to the gentleman.

Shelley was practically across the garage and headed for the stairs when she heard the gunshot.

She turned to see her friend running wildly towards her. Something had gone awfully wrong. Shelley looked back to see the woman standing over the old gentleman and screaming her head off. "Let's get out of here," shouted Shelley's partner. "What did you do?" Shelley winced, for she knew without being told that somehow the gun had gone off and possibly killed the old guy.

"Just let's get out of here," screamed her partner in crime. There was a waste bin just at the door. The gun was tossed in but there also was something else there - Shelley stared directly into the camera.

DISPOSITION HEARING

During a disposition hearing, the judge will determine the most appropriate form of treatment or custody for juvenile offenders.

Basically, the disposition hearing is the equivalent of the sentencing portion of an adult criminal case.

JUSTICE IS TEMPERED

Shelley's name was called by the court bailiff. She shuffles past her fellow inmates to the end of the row and into the aisle. The bailiff escorts her to the podium which stands directly in front of the judge's bench. There is no way to avert her eyes from those of Judge Stiffneck's. But before the judge hands out the court's punishment, there are two others in the court that Shelley hasn't noticed.

The old couple from the parking garage shooting was seated near the back of the court.

Thankfully, the old gentleman had only been grazed that night. The bullet went through his right thigh.

The old woman had asked to speak directly to the young lady who had disrupted their lives so on that frightening night. The couple rose and gently walked to the front of the courtroom. All eyes were on them and then on Shelley to see what her reactions would be.

Her husband - now on a walker - stood by his wife's side as she told of the harrowing night last Christmas. The courtroom gasped as she relayed the incidents of that fateful evening.

"Order in the court!"

But she wanted Shelley to know that while praying for the recovery of her husband, they had also prayed for the perpetrators – especially when they were told how young they were.

Shelley lowered her head in shame as the old woman talked of forgiveness. She also wanted Shelley's family to know that there was no animosity towards any of them and if there were anything that she and her husband could do for them, to just please somehow get in touch with them.

The courtroom was totally silent as the old gentleman began to speak. His voice was low and gravely and weak. He also told Shelley that his heart would not let him hate her and her friend for what they had done. He did tell of his ordeal – the long hospital stay, the therapy and the pain. He hoped that Shelley would turn her life around before it was impossible to do so.

 "That night in the garage there were two guardian angels – one for me and one for you. Mine kept the bullet from killing me and yours kept that same bullet from killing you. You would have just been another statistic of a wayward youth that finally fell completely down that dark rabbit hole. After speaking with the judge and others, I'm told that this is your last chance to move into a positive direction. There are plenty of people willing to help you, young lady, he said sternly – but you must want the help and reach out for it. I wish you Godspeed."

The judge asks Shelley if she has anything she would like to say to the couple or any remarks at all.

Shelley stares directly at the couple but she doesn't see them.

Shelley thinks about when she was a little girl and her mother spanked her for misbehaving. How she thought her mom was so mean. She thought of the way she had treated the young girl who had taken her own life. What part did she have in that? The stealing and breaking into another's property. Was any of it worth it? The fact that she was almost part of a murder. Can she or does she deserve forgiveness...

The judge loudly clears his throat.

Shelley sternly looks the judge in the eye and says, "I have nothing to say."

 And with that, the couple slowly proceeded to the back of the courtroom and out the doors. They had said their piece and were now going on with their lives.

JUDICIAL WAIVER

A judicial waiver occurs when a juvenile court judge transfers a case from juvenile to adult court to deny the juvenile the protections that juvenile jurisdictions provide. In most states, the youngest offender who can be waived to adult court is a 17 or 18-year old, although in some states, this age is as low as 13 or 14.

Usually, the offense allegedly committed must be particularly egregious for the case to be waived judicially, or there must be a long history of offenses.

Some states also have a legal provision which allows the prosecutor to file a juvenile case in both juvenile and adult court because the offense and the age of the accused meet certain criteria.

Transfer into an adult court proceeding can result in several negative consequences for the accused. Juvenile proceedings take place in a closed courtroom, while adult proceedings are typically public. A conviction record is generally sealed for juveniles, while adult records are frequently publicly accessible. Adult penalties tend to be much harsher than the penalties for the comparable juvenile offenses.

The juvenile courts tend to be focused on the rehabilitation of the accused, unlike adult courts which may be focused more on punishment.

SENTENCING

Judge Stiffneck has had quite some time to think about Shelley and her co-defendant over these last few months. He must take into account so many factors of this case before handing down his decision.

Shelley lost her father at very young age and has been raised solely by her mother. Caring for a child has always, in his mind, demanded a team effort. Shelley's mother has done the best she knows how under the circumstances, which, unfortunately, wasn't always enough. Shelley left school to run the streets – her mother had lost complete control.

Being bullied herself at a young age, Shelley was pushed into disruptive behavior as a defense mechanism. Judge Stiffneck gets that. But Shelley has had every opportunity to rise above her upbringing. She is not the first kid to have to overcome severe struggles in their lives. Most make a decent effort at trying to better themselves and get on the right path to success.

Shelley has been given numerous opportunities - Shelley is one of those kids that only time and experience will open her eyes - and then she will find that it's too late - she will be so far gone that escaping her new hell will be all but impossible to do.

Shelley showed zero remorse in the courtroom today. Even when her elderly victims
stood up for her, she showed hardly any re-
action, except to bow her head in shame.
But Shelley was only ashamed that her dirty
laundry was being presented in public for all
to see – there wasn't any real remorse.
Shelley is the typical defendant who is not
sorry for her actions, but only sorry she got
caught.

Sentencing children is always a difficult but
necessary task for juvenile judges. There is
sadness, for the family especially; a loss to
the community, as a whole; and a deep regret felt by the sentencing judges. Judge
Stiffneck is no exception.

Judge Stiffneck asked once again if Shelley
had anything she wanted to say – if not to
the victims, then surely to her mother.

Shelley stoically stared at Judge Stiffneck. The soft sobs of her mother could be heard throughout the courtroom.

Judge Stiffneck hands down his sentence:

Shelley and her co-defendant have been waived up to adult court.

FAQ'S (Frequently Asked Questions)

1.What is juvenile recidivism?

The term used for children under eighteen-years-old who habitually commit crimes. Juvenile habitual offenders often have mental issues that cause a repetition in criminal behavior

2. Can juvenile criminal records be expunged?

Different types of juvenile records can be expunged at different times. There used to be a mandatory wait until a youth's 18th birthday to file to expunge any part of the juvenile record. As of January 1st, 2017, some juvenile records are eligible to be expunged as soon as the matter is closed, even if youth is not 18 at the time.

3. Is there a cost for youth to stay in detention?

Most state statutes mandate the state and counties have a joint obligation to pay for the costs of secure detention care provided for juveniles. In some instances, there can be court-ordered fees families must pay for the cost of caring for their child while he is in DJJ's custody or under DJJ supervision.

4.What is pre-trial intervention?

Diversion – cases handled outside the court process with alternative consequences, like Teen Court. Teen court (sometimes called youth court or peer court) is a problem-solving court within the juvenile justice system where teens charged with certain types of offenses can be sentenced by a jury of same-aged peers.

5.What is electronic monitoring?

A GPS device worn around the ankle to make sure your child stays within court-ordered areas, usually only at home or school.

6. What is a misdemeanor?

A crime less serious than a felony.

7. What is a Pre-disposition Report?

A Juvenile Probation Officer's recommendation to the court about what should happen with your child's case based on assessments and information gathered.

8. What is being truant?

A student with 5 unexcused absences from school in one month or 10 in a 90-day period.

9.What is restitution?

When a judge orders a child to pay a victim (through the court) for damage done by a crime.

10. **Are families** allowed to visit juveniles detained in detention?

Yes. Visitation is an important component of a youth's stay in detention and is encouraged and supported by detention staff. Parents, grandparents, and legal guardians are approved visitors. A youth's assigned Juvenile Probation Officer (JPO) should be contacted to approve both visitation list additions and special visitation arrangements.

All visitors shall be denied entrance if they:

- ✓ Are disruptive or uncooperative;
- ✓ Refuse to be searched;
- ✓ Refuse to comply with officer instructions;
- ✓ Are under the influence or appear to be under the influence of any intoxicating substance;
- ✓ Fail to present proper photo identification;
- ✓ Attempt to introduce contraband to the secure area and/or;

✓ Are dressed in inappropriate attire as outlined in the Facility Operating Procedures and as posted at the facility entrance.

11. What happens to my son/daughter's personal property?

DJJ recognizes the need to safeguard the personal property of youth brought into its care. All the youth's property is inventoried at admission and the valuable property is stored in the facility safe. Other personal property (clothing, shoes, etc.) is stored in a locked storage room for the duration of the youth's stay. Property is to be released to the youth upon release from the facility.

12. What can we bring our son/daughter?

The detention center provides supplies and clothing for all youth. Detained youth are not permitted to have money. Gifts are discouraged while the detainee is in the detention center. Snacks are provided by the detention center every night. Detainee are not permitted to have any tobacco products at any time while they are in the detention center.

13. Can I bring them their medications?

Yes. Only medication in the original container from a licensed pharmacy, with an appropriate, current label intact on the medication container may be taken into the facility.

13. How long do juveniles stay in detention?

Juvenile detention is a short-term temporary program. Juveniles who require long-term sanctions and rehabilitation are placed into non-residential or residential treatment programs. If the judge continues the youth's detention status, his/her length of stay may extend up to 21 days or more.

BULLYING RESOURCES

- www.apa.org

- www.StopBullying.gov

- www.BullyingStatistics.org

- www.pacer.org

CHILDREN ADVOCACY GROUPS

1. *Boys and Girls Club*

2. *Big Brothers Big Sisters*

3. *National Child Advocacy Centers*

4. *The United Way - Character Playbook*

5. *Child and Family Services*

"it takes a village to raise a child"

NOTES

* 9 7 8 1 9 8 1 0 5 1 7 0 0 *